T0008374

To the Moss Family
—Lorna

For Emma
—Alice

Author's Acknowledgments

Joey loved his teams. Books are created by a team. Thanks to the Moss Family and Joey's sister Pattie Walker; the Edmonton Oilers organization and players: Wayne Gretzky, Barrie Stafford, Dan Cote-Rosen, and Connor McDavid; the Edmonton Football Club: Dwayne Mandrusiak; the Edmonton Down Syndrome Society: Rosalind Mosychuk; agent Amy Thomkins; Sleeping Bear Press: Heather Hughes, Jennifer Bacheller, Barb McNally for fine editing, and Alice Carter for her incredible representation of Joey.

SLEEPING BEAR PRESS™

Text Copyright © 2022 Lorna Schultz Nicholson
Illustration Copyright © 2022 Alice Carter
Design Copyright © 2022 Sleeping Bear Press
All rights reserved. No part of this book may be reproduced in any manner without the express written consent of the publisher, except in the case of brief excerpts in critical reviews and articles. All inquiries should be addressed to:
Sleeping Bear Press
2395 South Huron Parkway, Suite 200, Ann Arbor, MI 48104
www.sleepingbearpress.com © Sleeping Bear Press
Printed and bound in the United States.

10 9 8 7 6 5 4 3 2 1

Library of Congress Cataloging-in-Publication Data
Names: Schultz Nicholson, Lorna, author. | Moss, Joey, 1963-2020 | Carter, Alice, illustrator.
Title: Good morning, sunshine! : the Joey Moss story / Lorna Schultz Nicholson ; illustrated by Alice Carter.
Description: Ann Arbor, MI : Sleeping Bear Press, [2022] | Audience: Ages 4-8 |
Audience: Grades 2-3 | Summary: "The biography of Canadian Joey
Moss, a man born with Down syndrome who worked with the NHL Edmonton
Oilers hockey team, and was an inspiration for neurodiverse people and
an advocate for inclusivity"— Provided by publisher.
Identifiers: LCCN 2022003607 | ISBN 9781534111691 (hardcover)
Subjects: LCSH: Down syndrome—Patients—Alberta—Edmonton—Biography—Juvenile literature. |
Dementia—Patients—Alberta—Edmonton—Biography—Juvenile literature. |
Edmonton Oilers (Hockey team)—Employees—Juvenile literature.
Classification: LCC RC571 .S38 2022 | DDC 616.85/88420092
[B]—dc23/eng/20220202
LC record available at https://lccn.loc.gov/2022003607

GOOD MORNING, SUNSHINE!

THE JOEY MOSS STORY

LORNA SCHULTZ NICHOLSON

ILLUSTRATED BY ALICE CARTER

PUBLISHED by SLEEPING BEAR PRESS™

JOEY MOSS LOVED MAKING PEOPLE SMILE.

He made people smile when he played the tambourine.

He made people smile when he sang "O Canada" with his hand across his heart.

And he made people smile when he danced to the song "La Bamba."

But most of all, Joey Moss made people smile just by being himself.

Joseph (Joey) Neil Moss was born on September 25, 1963,
in Edmonton, Alberta, Canada.

When Joey was born, he had seven brothers and four sisters!
He was the twelfth child for Sophie and Lloyd Moss.

When his parents brought Joey home from the hospital,
they knew there was something different about him. He was born with Down syndrome.

Down syndrome is a genetic disorder, and Joey was born with an extra chromosome in his DNA.
This meant that Joey might have delays in development and learn differently.

In 1963, children born with Down syndrome were often institutionalized, which meant they did not live at home with their families. Parents were told their child would be a burden.

But Joey's parents didn't listen. They kept him at home and treated him like all his siblings.

At dinnertime, his mother would quickly rattle off their names:

Mervin,

Terry,

Pattie,

Mickey,

Timmy,

Jimmy,

Suzie,

Barbie,

Freddie,

Mark,

Vikki,

Joey.

Five years later, Stephen was born,
making thirteen children total.

The Moss family led a humble but happy life. They loved music and even had their own band called the Alaska Highway Birthquakes. Everyone played musical instruments and sang. Mr. Moss thought that his family could be like the von Trapp family in *The Sound of Music*.

The family travelled to performances in an old bus that had been fixed up. The back of the bus was filled with saxophones, trumpets, drums, accordions, a base fiddle, and sometimes even a piano.

They mostly played in small-town community halls and event centers.
At the age of three, Joey had his performance debut. Before Joey went onstage,
his father handed him a tambourine.

Once Joey heard the music, he danced and shook his tambourine.
The crowd applauded enthusiastically. From then on,
Joey loved performing and making people smile.

Eventually, as the older children graduated and moved away from home, the family stopped touring.

Joey attended school but not with his brothers and sisters.
He attended the Winnifred Stewart School. At the time, children born with
Down syndrome and other developmental disabilities didn't go to regular
school. Winnifred Stewart created this school for children like her own son.
It was the first school of its kind in Canada.

Winnifred Stewart

Certificate
Graduation
awarded to
Joey Moss
June 23, 1980
Winnifred Stew

In 1977, when Joey was fourteen and living at home with five of his siblings, his father died. Suddenly Mrs. Moss was a single mother. Money was tight and the family faced some hardships. They even had to move from their home.

But Mrs. Moss made sure Joey stayed in school.
He graduated when he was almost seventeen.

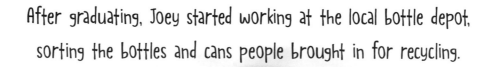

After graduating, Joey started working at the local bottle depot,
sorting the bottles and cans people brought in for recycling.

Joey was glad to have a job, but it wasn't much fun
and it wasn't easy for him to get to the depot.

Joey had to catch several buses. He did this all on his own by memorizing the bus numbers. Joey worked at the depot for several years.

But then things changed.

One cold, snowy day, a hockey player named Wayne Gretzky saw Joey shivering at the bus station on his way to the depot. Wayne played in the National Hockey League (NHL) for the Edmonton Oilers team, and he was a friend of the Moss family.

He knew how hard Joey worked at the bottle depot,
and Wayne wanted him to have a job that made him happier.
So Wayne asked Glen Sather, the general manager of the Edmonton Oilers,
if the team would hire Joey to work in the equipment room.

Mr. Sather agreed!

Joey started working with the Edmonton Oilers during the 1984–1985 NHL season as a dressing room attendant. He folded towels, vacuumed and cleaned the dressing room, filled water bottles, and carried the players' sticks to the bench.

Joey prided himself on being a good worker.

The players and staff liked him, but not everyone was kind at first.

Once, as Joey was pulling towels out of the dryer, he heard people talking about him, saying hurtful things. Hearing their words, Joey got angry.

"I'm not stupid!" he said, standing up for himself. He knew it was important to speak up.

The players liked Joey's work ethic and outgoing personality, and they made him feel like part of the team.

Joey enjoyed his job, but he liked doing more. He wanted to make everyone feel good. When a player or staff member arrived for practice, he greeted them with a big smile and "Good morning, sunshine!"

Joey worked hard, but he also had fun.

Joey loved watching wrestling on television and he would often pretend-wrestle with the players. They even got him a real wrestling belt to keep in the dressing room. Whoever won the pretend match earned the belt.

An NHL season is long, with many practices and games. Joey's playful jokes and cheerful personality helped keep team spirits up.

If a new player joined the team, Joey wrestled against him
as part of his welcome to the club!

Before the start of Oilers home games, Joey would put his hand to his heart and sing "O Canada." He was so enthusiastic in his singing that the cameras would show him on the jumbotron!

The fans cheered and players like Wayne Gretzky, Mark Messier, and Kevin Lowe would glance up and watch. His presence inspired them for the puck drop.

Joey did such a good job with the Oilers that in 1986, the Canadian Football League (CFL) Edmonton team asked him to work there, too.

Because Joey worked for both teams, he was often seen at events. Joey became a famous face in Edmonton. When he walked down the street, cars would honk and people would shout out,

"Hey, there's Joey Moss!"

HONK HONK

SHOP LOCAL

In restaurants, he was asked to sign autographs.

Joey Moss

As Joey became a celebrity in Edmonton, he was often asked to attend many charity events. He was happy to help out in his community. Everyone loved seeing his smiling face and he was always lots of fun to be around. He often sang the national anthem—he even sang at the Alberta Legislature.

At charity golf tournaments, he would sign autographs. Then he would hit the ball off a tee and see if anyone could outdrive him. If he missed, he tried again.

At the Edmonton Down Syndrome Society fashion show,
Joey walked the stage as a model and even danced his own moves as the music played.

Like everyone else, Joey enjoyed his birthday. And when he turned fifty, he had several parties to celebrate!

One very special party was hosted by the Oilers. It took place in the backyard of Ryan Smyth, who was an assistant captain of the Oilers at that time. A real wrestling ring was set up and pro wrestlers came. When Joey was called to the ring to wrestle one of the pros, he wore an orange cape and a blue wrestling mask. At the end of the match, they announced him the winner.

The players hoisted him over their heads and sang "Happy Birthday."

FOR THE REST OF HIS LIFE, JOEY MOSS
CONTINUED TO BE AN INSPIRATION FOR PEOPLE AND
AN ADVOCATE FOR THOSE WITH DISABILITIES.

JUST BY BEING HIMSELF, JOEY SHOWED THE WORLD
THAT EVERYONE CAN BE A FORCE FOR GOOD,
ACTIVE IN THEIR COMMUNITY, AND A POSITIVE ROLE MODEL.

JOEY MOSS retired from the Oilers when he was in his fifties, after he had been diagnosed with early onset dementia. He had worked for the organization for thirty years, longer than any hockey player.

In July 2020, Joey was having fun and dancing in his room at the Winnifred Stewart House when he fell and broke his hip. An ambulance came and as he was being put on the stretcher, Joey blew kisses to the people around him. Even injured, Joey was doing what he did best—making people smile.

On October 26, 2020, with his family by his side, Joey Moss passed away. He was fifty-seven years old.

JOEY'S LEGACY LIVES ON!

Joey showed the world that people born with Down syndrome could be active in their communities. He was an advocate for those with disabilities. He did so many things to help bring awareness and compassion to people like himself so they would be treated better in society and be given more opportunities.

In 1988 the Joey's Home Trust was created by the Winnifred Stewart Foundation. Wayne Gretzky started the trust by hosting golf tournaments to raise funds. Additional funding was raised by other events. In nine years, enough was raised to build Joey's Home, a residential facility for people with disabilities. The original Joey's Home has eight rooms for those residents who need assistance, and four for those who live independently. Now there are several Joey's Homes throughout Edmonton.

The Empties to Winn program began in 2006 in support of the Winnifred Stewart Foundation and Joey's Home. Joey promoted the Empties program on the radio and at events, encouraging businesses to place special blue bins in their offices to collect empties. Trucks featuring Joey's smiling face drive around Edmonton and the surrounding area to pick up the empties.

For nine straight years Joey attended the Edmonton Police Service's Lifestyle Camp for at-risk youth. He was asked back year after year because the campers loved having him around.

The city of Edmonton celebrated and honoured Joey for his work on behalf of people with disabilities. In 2007 he was given the Mayor's Award and in 2008 a giant mural of Joey was painted near 99 Street.

And then there is the Joey Moss Cup! Since 2010, on their last day of training camp, the Edmonton Oilers have had an inter-squad game, playing for the Joey Moss Cup. Fans pay to watch, with proceeds presented partly to the Winnifred Stewart Foundation in support of the Joey's Home Trust and partly to the University of Alberta in support of the Golden Bears hockey program. When he was able to participate, Joey loved going on the ice to present the trophy to the winning team.

One very special posthumous honour will take place in the fall of 2022. A new elementary school called the Joey Moss School will open in Edmonton. Joey would have been very proud.

A NOTE FROM THE AUTHOR

Joey was an amazing soul, and I am a better person because I knew him. I was lucky to have been able to dance with him (yes, to "La Bamba") and enjoy his company at various events. He always brought the fun factor to any occasion. To celebrate Joey's fifty-fifth birthday, I attended the opening of the Joey Moss Literacy Centre for Excellence in Edmonton. This facility gives children born with Down syndrome help with their reading skills. As an author, literacy is important to me; a percentage of my royalties from this book will go to this legacy of Joey's. Even from above, Joey is still helping others be better, myself included. I was honoured to write his story!

"JOEY WAS GIVEN LOVE AND HE GAVE LOVE BACK."
—Pattie Walker (Joey's oldest sister)

"JOEY MADE OUR LIVES BETTER."
—Wayne Gretzky (former NHL Edmonton Oilers captain)

"HE BRIGHTENED UP THE DAY!"
—Connor McDavid (NHL Edmonton Oilers player)

JOEY'S HONOURS AND AWARDS!
★ NHL Alumni Association's Seventh Man Award, 2003
★ Edmonton Mayor's Services for Persons with Disabilities Award, 2007
★ Queen Elizabeth II Diamond Jubilee Medal, 2012
★ Inducted into the Alberta Sports Hall of Fame, 2015
★ Marlin Styner Achievement Award, 2015– Alberta Premier Council Award
★ Inducted into the Hall of Fame for Professional Hockey Athletic Trainers Society, 2017
★ The Joey Moss Literacy Centre for Excellence was created in 2018